There's sumpm funny goin' on.
Awraht?

Don't ast me.
Tuhn the page toreckly.
'N see fo' yo' sef.

HOW TO SPEAK SOUTHERN

by Southerners
about Southerners and for Southerners
(Yankees, too).

HOW TO SPEAK SOUTHERN

by Steve Mitchell
with illustrations by
SCRAWLS (Sam C. Rawls)

BANTAM BOOKS
TORONTO · NEW YORK · LONDON · SYDNEY

*This low-priced Bantam Book
has been completely reset in a type face
designed for easy reading, and was printed
from new plates. It contains the complete
text of the original hard-cover edition.*
NOT ONE WORD HAS BEEN OMITTED.

HOW TO SPEAK SOUTHERN

*A Bantam Book / published by arrangement with
the authors*

PRINTING HISTORY

Palm Beach Newspapers edition published October 1976
2nd printing .... *November 1976*

Bantam edition / November 1976

2nd printing ... December 1976	11th printing .... July 1977
3rd printing .... December 1976	12th printing .... September 1977
4th printing .... December 1976	13th printing .... November 1977
5th printing ...... January 1977	14th printing .... March 1978
6th printing ...... January 1977	15th printing ...... October 1978
7th printing ...... January 1977	16th printing .... February 1979
8th printing .... February 1977	17th printing .... June 1979
9th printing .... March 1977	18th printing .... December 1979
10th printing .... May 1977	19th printing .... April 1980

20th printing .... *September 1980*

Back cover photo by Guy Ferrell.

ISBN 0-553-14611-4

Published simultaneously in the United States and Canada

Bantam Books are published by Bantam Books, Inc. Its trademark, consisting of the words ''Bantam Books'' and the por-
trayal of a bantam, is Registered in U.S. Patent and Trademark
Office and in other countries. Marca Registrada. Bantam
Books, Inc., 666 Fifth Avenue, New York, New York 10103.

PRINTED IN THE UNITED STATES OF AMERICA

29 28 27 26

This book is dedicated to all Yankees
in the hope that it will
teach them how to talk right.

A

Ah: The things you see with, and the personal pronoun denoting individuality. "Ah think Ah've got somethin' in mah ah."

Ahmoan: An expression of intent. "Ahmoan have a little drink. You want one?"

Aig: A breakfast food that may be fried, scrambled, boiled or poached. "Which came first, the chicken or the aig?"

Ail: To be ill or afflicted by something. "That mule sure is actin' strange. Wonder what ails him?"

OLD ARN   NEW ARN

Aint: The sister of your mother or father. "Son go over and give Aint Bea a big hug."

Airish: Drafty, cool. "Don't leave that door open. It's too airish already."

Airs: Mistakes. "That shortstop's made two airs, and the game's not half over yet."

Argy: To dispute in a contentious manner. "Ah told you to take your bath, boy, and Ah'm not gonna stand here and argy with you about it."

Arn: An electrical instrument used to remove wrinkles from clothing.

"Ah'm not gonna arn today. It's too hot."

Arshtaters: A staple of the Irish diet and the source of French fries. "Ah like arshtaters, but Ah hate to peel 'em."

Ast: To interrogate or inquire, as when a revenue agent seeks information about illegal moonshine stills. "Don't ast me so many questions. It makes me mad."

Attair: Contraction used to indicate the specific item desired. "Pass me attair gravy, please."

Awduh: A state of affairs that depends on obedience to law. "The

marshal brought law and awduh to this town."

Awf: The opposite of on. "Take your muddy feet awf the table."

Awfis: The place where men say they have to work late and sometimes actually do. "Go ahead and have supper without me, honey. Ah have to work late at the awfis."

Awl: An amber fluid used to lubricate engines. "Ah like that car, but it sure does use a lot of awl."

Awraht: Okay. "If you want to go back home to your mother, that's awraht with me."

AY-rab: The desert people who

inhabit much of North Africa but not much of Israel. "That fella looks like a AY-rab, don't he?"

B

Bad off: Desperately in need of, also extremely ill. 1. "Is that *Valley of the Dolls?* You must be bad off for somethin' to read." 2. "Jim's in the hospital. He's bad off."

Bad to: Inclined toward, prone to. "Johnny's bad to get in fights when he gets drunk."

Bait: A surfeit of. "Ah hope you get a bait of them spareribs, 'cause you've et about all of 'em."

Bard: To obtain the use of, not

always on a temporary basis. "He bard mah shovel and never did bring it back."

Batry: A boxlike device that produces electricity. "Looks like your car's got a dead batry."

Bawl: What water does at 212 degrees Fahrenheit. "That gal can't even bawl water without burnin' it."

Beholden: Indebted to. "Ah'm beholden to you for loanin' me that five dollars."

Bidness: The art of selling something for more than you paid for it. "My cousin Archie is in the real estate bidness."

Bleeve: Expression of intent or faith. "Ah bleeve we ought to go to church this Sunday."

Bobbuh: One who cuts hair. "Ah wish you'd go to a different bobbuh."

Bobbycue: A delectable Southern sandwich that is prepared properly only in certain parts of North Carolina. It consists of chopped pork, cole slaw and a fiery sauce made chiefly of vinegar, red pepper and ketchup. "Four bobbycues to go, please."

Body: Person, usually an oblique reference to yourself. "A body can't get a minute's peace around this house."

Bound to: Certain to. "Too much beer is bound to give you a hangover."

Break bad: To behave in a violent, wanton or outrageous manner for no discernible reason. "Ole Bill broke bad last night and wound up in jail."

Break of: To induce the abandonment of an undesirable trait or habit: "Ah'm gonna break that husband of mine of lyin' to me if it's the last thing Ah do."

Bub: A fragile glass object that converts electricity into illumination. "Ah think that light bub's burnt out."

Bum: An explosive device dropped from airplanes called bummers. "Ah think we ought to drop the atomic bum on 'em."

Bumminham: The biggest city in Alabama. "You can travel cross this entire land, they ain't no place like Bumminham."

C

Caint: Cannot. "Ah just caint understand why this checkbook won't balance."

Carry: To convey from one place to another, usually by automobile. "Can you carry me down to the store in yo' car?"

Cent: The plural of cent. "You paid five dollars for that necktie? Ah wouldn't give fifty cent for it."

Cheer: A piece of furniture used for setting. "Pull up a cheer and set a spell."

Chimbley: What smoke comes out of. "Ah bleeve that chimbley's stopped up."

Co-cola: The soft drink that started in Atlanta and conquered the world. "Ah hear they even sell Co-cola in Russia."

Comin' up a cloud: An approaching storm. "Stay close to the house. It's comin' up a cloud."

Commite nigh: To come very close to. "When Sue-Ann caught her husband kissin' that waitress from the Blue Moon, she commite nigh killin' him."

Costes: The price of something. "Don't buy lettuce if it costes too much."

Crine: Weeping. "What's that girl crine about?"

Cuss: Profane language or a malediction. "The Hope Diamond has got a cuss on it."

Cut awf: To switch off. "It's too bright in here, honey. Why don't we cut awf that light bub?"

Cut the fool: To behave in a silly or foolish manner. "Quit cuttin' the fool and do your homework."

Cyst: To render aid. "Can Ah cyst you with those packages, ma'am?"

D

Dawfins: Name of the professional football team in Miami. "You think the Dawfins can win the conference this year?"

Dawg: A four-legged animal much esteemed in rural sections of the South. "Ah just don't feel right unless Ah got a couple of huntin' dawgs around the house."

Darest: Old English contraction of dare not, meaning unadvisable to. "You darest talk about the stock market around your daddy since he lost all that money in it."

Dayum: A cuss word Rhett Butler used in *Gone With the Wind*. "Frankly, my dear, I don't give a dayum."

Dinner: The meal Southerners eat while Northerners are eating lunch. When the Northerners are eating dinner, Southerners are eating supper. "We're just havin' butterbeans and biscuits for dinner, but we'll have a big supper."

Doc: A condition caused by an absence of light. "It's mighty doc in here."

Done: 1. Finished. "Are you done eatin'?" 2. Already. "Has the bus done gone?"

Draw up: To contract or shrink. "Ah told you that blouse would draw up if you washed it in hot water."

Drank: To consume a liquid. "You want a drank of this Co-cola?"

E

Earl: A metal device used to improve radio and television reception. "You could pick up a lot more stations if you had a higher TV earl."

MAMA MIA, YOU DON'TA HAVE TO BE EYETALYUN TO ENJOYA SPAGHET, YAWL.

Eat up with: Excessively afflicted by. "That woman's jest eat up with jealousy."

Et: To have eaten. "You done et?"

Etlanna: The city General Sherman burned during the War for Southern Independence. "Etlanna is kind of like New York with pecan trees."

Everwhichaways: To be scattered in all directions. "You should have been there when the train hit that chicken truck. Them chickens flew everwhichaways."

Eyetalyun: A native of Italy or an American ethnic group of that heri-

tage. "You don't have to be Eyetalyun to like spaghetti."

F

Far: A state of combustion that
produces heat and light. "Ah reckon
it's about time to put out the far and
call in the dawgs."

Fatback: Salt pork—an essential
ingredient in the cooking of collard
greens and beans. "Ah like fried-out
fatback as much as bacon."

Fault: To place blame. "You can't
fault a man for takin' a little drank of
liquor once in a while."

Favor: To resemble. "That boy sure

SAY IT WITH FLARES

does favor his daddy, don't he?"

Fayan: An electrical applicance that circulates air. "It's hot in here. Cut on that fayan."

Fem: A necessary ingredient in the creation of photographs. "Are you sure you got fem in that camera?"

Fixin: Preparing to. "Ah'm fixin to dig me some worms and go fishin.'"

Flares: The colorful, sweet-smelling part of a plant. "If yo wife's mad at you, it's smart to take her some flares."

Fur piece: A considerable distance. "It's a fur piece from here to Jacksonville."

G

Give up to be: Generally conceded to be. "He's give up to be the crookedest lawyer in the whole state of Mississippi."

Git: To acquire. "If you're goin' to the store, git me a six-pack of beer."

Git by with: To get away with. "You think your wife's gonna believe that story? You'll never git by with it."

Git shed of: To rid oneself of. "That car is costin' me too much money, and Ah'm gonna git shed of it."

Goff: A game played with clubs and a little white ball, usually to the accompaniment of much profanity. "Ah hate goff."

"JEST A GOOD OLE BOY"

Goobers: Peanuts. "It's fun to put goobers in a Co-cola and watch it foam."

Good ole boy: Any Southern male between the ages of 16 and 60 who has an amiable disposition and is fond of boon companions, strong drink, hound dawgs, fishin', huntin' and good-lookin' women, but not necessarily in that order. "Basil's a good ole boy."

Go to: Intend. "You shouldn't have whipped Jimmy for breakin' that window. He didn't go to do it."

Go to the bad: To spoil. "Put that mayonnaise back in the refrigerator

WHY, THEM'S GRIYUTS, HONEY.

or it'll go to the bad."

Gracious plenty: Enough or more than enough. "Don't let me eat any more of that country ham. I've had a gracious plenty."

Griyuts: What no Southern breakfast would be complete without—grits. "Ah like griyuts with butter and sawt on 'em, but Ah purely love 'em with red-eye gravy."

Guff: An oil company. "Where's the high school? Well, you go down this road for two blocks and turn left at the Guff station ..."

Gull: A female. "She's just about the sweetest, prettiest gull in town."

H

Haint: A ghost, spirit or apparition. "If you walk past the graveyard at midnight, you might see a haint."

Hale: Where General Sherman is going for what he did to Etlanna. "General Sherman said 'War is hale', and he made sure it was."

Hard: To secure employment. "Ah didn't get that job. They hard somebody else."

Hawg: A noble and eminently edible animal which furnishes Southerners with such delicacies as country ham, spareribs, fatback, fried pork skins, pickled pig's feet

and chopped pork for barbecue. "When it gits to be cold weather, you know it's time to kill hawgs."

Heepa: A great deal of. "You in a heepa trouble, boy."

Hep: To aid or benefit. "Ah can't hep it if Ah'm still in love with you."

Hern (and Hisn): Feminine possessive and the opposite of hisn. "Is that blonde hair really hern?"

Hey: Salutation used by Southerners in lieu of hello or hi. "Hey, Bill. Where you been lately?"

Hyuh: Word used to summon dawgs. "Hyuh, boy, hyuh!"

I

Idinit: Term employed by genteel Southerners who wish to avoid saying "Ain't." "Mighty hot today, idinit?"

Idy: Idea. "Have you got any idy the tricks that dawg can do?"

In a manner: A baffling redundancy sometimes inserted into a sentence. "That baby acts like its starvin' in a manner to death," meaning the baby appears hungry.

J

Jawja: Southern state just north of Florida. "Sherman burnt Etlanna when he marched through Jawja."

Jevver: Did you ever. "Jevver hear anything so dumb in your life?"

Jew: Did you. "Jew want to buy that comic book, son, or just stand there and read it here?"

K

Keer: To be concerned. "That girl don't keer nothin' about him."

Kindly: Sort of. "When Ed's line broke and he lost that big bass, he just looked kindly pale and sick."

Kumpny: Guests. "Be home on time. We're havin' kumpny for supper."

L

Lahf: The opposite of death. "Nobody said lahf was going to be easy."

Laht: The opposite of dark. "We need more laht in here."

Law: Police, or as Southerners pronounce it, POleece. "We better get out of here. That bartender's done called the law."

Lawst: To be unsure of one's location. "This road don't go nowhere. We're lawst."

Least one: Smallest. Generally used in reference to children. "Johnny's my oldest, and Sue Ann is the least one."

LIGHT BREAD

BISCUIT

CORN BREAD

(REAL BREAD)

Lectricty: What the power company won't turn on without a deposit to make sure you pay your lectric bill. "That air conditioner sure uses a lot of lectricity."

Let on: To indicate knowledge of, either by word or action. "Her husband's been drunk for 10 years, but don't let on you know anything about it."

Libel: Likely to. "If your wife finds out you're runnin' around with that go-go dancer, she's libel to kill you."

Lick: A blow. "You and Billy got in a fight? Who passed the first lick?"

Light bread: A pre-sliced loaf of soft, store-bought bread that no

WHOOEEE, NOW THAT'S LIKKER!!

Southern woman would have dared to place before her family in older and simpler times. "Git this light bread off the table, woman, and fix me some hot biscuits."

Like to: Almost. "When Ah saw she had on the same dress I did, Ah like to died."

Likker: Whisky; either the amber kind bought in stores or the home-made white kind the federal authorities frown upon. "Does he drink? Listen, he spills more likker than most people drink."

M

Ma'am (and Suh): Archaic terms

of courtesy and respect Southern children once were taught to use when addressing their elders. "Now when you talk to your teacher, you make sure you say 'Yes, ma'am' and 'No, ma'am', you hear me?"

Madge: A state of wedlock that any preacher can put you into, but only a lawyer can get you out of. "Seems like a lot of madges end in divorce these days."

Mah: Possessive personal pronoun. "Anybody seen mah huntin' boots?"

Mash: To press, as in the case of an elevator button. "Want me to mash yo floor for you, Ma'am?"

Mast: A disguise over part of the face. "Who was that mast man?" "Why, that was the Lone Ranger."

Mere: A reflective glass. "Mere, mere on the wall, who's the fairest of them all?"

Mess: A quantity of, usually enough for a meal. "That's a nice mess of fish."

Mite could: Might possibly. "If you'd invest in real estate you mite could make a lot of money."

Mind: To obey. "Now you mind yo big sister while Ah'm at the store, you hear?"

Miz: Southern form of address

stolen by the Women's Liberation movement. "Is that Miz Thompson comin' down the street?"

Moanin': Between daybreak and noon. "Good moanin', Suh."

Mommocked up: Damaged or defaced. "Don't try to paint the table with that old stiff brush. You'll jest get it mommocked up."

Muchablige: Thank you. "Muchablige for the lift, mister."

Munts: The 12 units into which the calendar year is divided. "Ah hadn't seen Bob in about three munts."

N

Nairn: Not any; not a one. "Ah'd

offer you a cigarette, but Ah don't have nairn."

Nawthun: Anything that is not Southern. "He is a classic product of the superior Nawthun educational system." (Sarcasm)

Nome: A child's negative reply to a female adult's question. "Jimmy, did you pull that cat's tail?" "Nome."

Not about to: To have no intention of. "Ah'm not about to pay $5,000 for a new car."

Nyawlins: The largest city in Louisiana (pronounced Loosyana). "Nyawlins is a nice town if you got a lot of money."

O

Oakree: A ridged, elongated vegetable known to the few Yankees who know about it as okra. "Ah don't like oakree any way but fried in flour with corn bread."

Orta: Should. "You orta see her in that bikini."

Ose: A type of car produced by General Motors. "That '55 Ose was the best car Ah ever had."

Ovair: In that direction. "Where's yo Daddy, son?" "He's ovair, suh."

Own: Opposite of awf. "Cut own the radio and let's listen to some music."

NEVER UNDERESTIMATE THE PARE OF A WOMAN

P

Papuh: What you write on; also, the colloquial term for newspaper. "Which papuh do you take?"

Pare: Strength, authority. "Never underestimate the pare of a woman."

Penny one: None at all, nothing. "He's been owin' me five dollars for five years, and Ah have yet to see penny one of it."

Peppuh: A hot spice widely used to season food. "Pass the peppuh, please."

Peyun: A writing instrument. "Some rob you with a six-gun, and some

with a fountain peyun."

Phrasin: Very cold. "Shut that door. It's phrasin in here."

Picayunish: Overly fastidious, picky. "That little blood spot won't hurt that egg. Don't be so picayunish."

Picked up: To have gained weight. "You've picked up a little, haven't you?"

Pentoes: Reddish-brown beans that constitute a staple of Southern diet because they get better every time they're reheated. "Ah druther have hot biscuits and a big plate of pentoes than steak."

Pitcher: An image, either drawn or photographed. "That's a good pitcher of Brenda Sue."

Play like: To pretend. "You play like you're the nurse and I'll be the doctor."

Plum: Completely. "Ah'm plum wore out."

Poke: A brown paper bag. "What's in that poke—lunch or liquor?"

PO-leece: One or more law enforcement officers. "Ah was jest standin' there mindin' my own bidness, judge, when this here PO-leece come up to me..."

Pore: 1. Destitute. "They're as pore

as church mice." 2. Inferior or sec-
ond-rate. "A pore excuse is better
than none."

Pot likker: The rich liquid left in the
pot after the greens have been
cooked for several hours. May be
drunk or sopped up with biscuits.
"Pot likker is full of vitamins and
minerals."

Prolly: Likely to. "Ah'll prolly go to
Etlanna this weekend."

Pupwood: A soft wood used in the
manufacture of papuh. "He's got
about a thousand acres of good
pupwood to sell."

Q

Quare: Strange, peculiar. "Ole Virgil's been actin' quare ever since that mule kicked him in the head."

Quietus: Pronounced kwi-EET-us and meaning to bring to an abrupt halt. "He was runnin' around with that blonde waitress from the Blue Moon Cafe 'til his wife found out about it and put the quietus on it."

R

Ratcheer: On this spot. "jest put the groceries down ratcheer."

Reckon: An expression of supposition or intent. "Where do you reckon he got that plaid suit?"

Rench: To wash off soapy water with clear water. "Ah'll wash the dishes if you'll rench 'em."

Rernt: Ruined. "That boy's drove that car so rough he's plum rernt it."

Retch: To grasp for. "The right fielder retch over into the stands and caught the ball."

Richmun: The capital of the Confederacy that exists today only because General Sherman ran out of matches. "He's hanging around that girl like Grant hung around Richmun."

Right smart: A goodly amount.

ROBUT E. LEE: THE FINEST GENTLEMAN WHO EVER DREW BREATH...

"She's put on a right smart of weight lately."

Robut E. Lee: The finest gentleman who ever drew breath and the greatest military leader since Julius Caesar and Alexander the Great. "Robut E. Lee didn't surrender. Grant just stole his sword and Lee was too much of a gentleman to ast him to give it back."

Rostenears: Fresh corn suitable for roasting or boiling. "Go over to the cornfield and pick me a dozen nice rostenears."

S

Saar: The opposite of sweet.

WHOOOEE... THAT'S SAAR

"These pickles are too saar."

Sandy Claws: The fat jolly man who comes down the chimbley every Christmas. "Did Sandy Claws bring you a lot of presents?"

Sawt: The ocean is full of it, and so is country ham. "Lot's wife looked back at Sodom and Gomorrah and turned into a pillar of sawt."

Scupter: One who makes statues out of rock. "Michelangelo was a good scupter."

Sebmup: Soft drink similar to ginger ale. "You want a Co-cola or a Sebmup?"

Shalot: The biggest city in Nawth Calina. "People who live in Shalot are called Shalotteans."

Shawt: The opposite of long. "She likes Willie, but she thinks he's too shawt for her."

Show: Certainly. "It show is hot today."

Shovelay: A General Motors car. "Nobody could drive a Shovelay like Junior Johnson."

Shurf: A county's chief law enforcement officer. "The shurf's raidin' bootleg joints again. Must be an election year."

Sinner: The exact middle of. "Have you been out to that new shoppin' sinner?"

Skase: Hard to find; in very short supply. "During the waw [war], sugar was skase."

Smore: An additional amount. "Want smore corn bread?"

Sorry: Lazy, shiftless. "That woman's so sorry she won't even make hot biscuits."

Spear: The opposite of inferior. "Ah couldn't get no satisfaction from that clerk, so Ah asked to see her immediate spear."

Spect: To imagine or suppose. "Ah spect a girl as sweet and pretty as she is could have 'bout any man she wanted."

Spittin image: Southern pronunciation of "spirit and image," meaning similarity of appearance. "She's the spittin image of her mother."

Standin in need of: Another

YANKEE SUGAR

SOUTHERN SUGAR

redundancy thrown in for no other reason than Southerners love rolling rhetoric and extravagant language. It simply means to need or want. "Ah'm standin in need of a cold beer."

Stow: Place where things are sold. "Son, Ah want you to go to the stow and get me some bakin' powder."

Studyin: Having an interest in, usually expressed negatively. "She said Ah wanted to date Homer? Ah'm not studyin that boy."

Subject to: Inclined in the direction of; prone to. "Tom's a good ole boy, but he's subject to get drunk every now and then."

Sugar: A kiss. "Come here and give

your momma some sugar."

Summers: Somewhere. "Ah know that boy's around here summers."

Sumpm: Something. "There's sumpm funny goin' on."

Suthun: The opposite of Nawthun. "Blackeyed peas and collard greens are Suthun dishes."

Swimmy-headed: Dizzy. "Don't drink that ice water so fast. It'll make you swimmy-headed."

Switch: Slender branch of a tree employed in the behavior modification of children. "Ah'm gonna cut me a switch and wear that boy out."

T

Tacky: An expression used exclusively by Southern females and almost always in regard to wearing apparel. Can mean anything from unfashionable to downright ugly. "Did you see that dress she was wearin'? Honey, it was so tacky..."

Tahm: A Yankee dictionary defines it as "A nonspatial continuum in which events occur in apparently irreversible succession from the past through the present to the future." Let's just say you either have too much of it or not enough. "It takes a long tahm to read the Sunday New York *Tahms*."

Tar: A round inflatable object that sometimes goes flat. "You shouldn't drive that car without a spare tar."

Tarred: Fatigued. "Ah'm too tarred to go bowlin' tonight."

Tar arn: Tool employed in changing

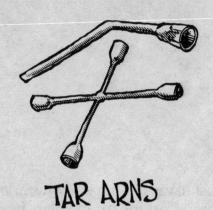

TAR ARNS

wheels. "You can't change a tar without a tar arn."

Tawk: A method of communication that still flourishes in the South in spite of television. "How come people from up Nawth say we tawk funny when they're the ones who tawk funny?"

Thang: A word Yankees consistently mispronounce as "Theeng." "Have you seen Sue Ann's new boyfriend? Honey, he's just the cutest thang."

Thow: To hurl. "Quick, thow me the ball!"

Toreckly: Later. "You go on ahead. We'll be along toreckly."

Tote: To carry. "Can you tote that big sack of corn meal?"

U

Ugly: Unpleasant, disagreeable or mean. "Now, Junior, don't you be ugly to your new sister."

Uhmurkin: Someone who lives in the United States of Uhmurka. "Thomas Jefferson was a great Uhmurkin."

Unnuther: One more. "You want unnuther biscuit?"

V

Vampar: A fearsome creature that sleeps in a coffin and lives on human blood. "Dracula was a vampar."

ViEENer: Small canned sausages. "You want smore viEENers?"

W

Waller: Rolling about, usually done by children and hogs. "Billy, don't you waller all over that bed. Ah jest made it up."

War: Metal strands attached to posts to enclose domestic animals. "Be careful and don't get stuck on that bob war."

Warshrag: A cloth used for cleaning people or dishes. "Hang up that warshrag when you're done with it."

Wawst: A stinging insect. "Watch out! That's a wawst, and he's mad as a hornet!"

Wenderlight: A pane of glass. "That baseball went right through the wenderlight."

Whitleather: A durable hide used for making harnesses and employed in speech for comparative purposes. "This steak's as tough as whitleather."

Whirr: Where. "Whirr you goin'?"

Whup: To beat up or to strike. "If a man kicks my dawg, he'll have to whup me."

Wore out: Exhausted, used up. "No use tryin' to fix that washing machine. It's plum wore out."

Wretched: A man's name. "Wretched Burton's a good actor."

Wuf: A fierce wild animal that is

closely related to the dog. When they get together it is called a wuf-pack, which is also the nickname of North Carolina State's athletic teams. "Ah never will forget the time the Wufpack whupped the tar out of UCLA and won the national basketball championship."

Wuk: Something most of us have to do to earn money. "Does he still wuk in Etlanna?"

Y

Yale: What Confederate soldiers did when they charged. "You wanna hear a Rebel yale?"

Yo: The possessive of you. "What's yo name?"

Yankee: Anyone who is not from Kentucky, Virginia, Tennessee,

YANKEE DIME

North Carolina, South Carolina, Georgia, Florida, Alabama, Mississippi, Louisiana, Arkansas, Texas and possibly Oklahoma and West-by-God-Virginia. A Yankee may become an honorary Southerner, but a Southerner cannot become a Yankee, assuming any Southerner wanted to. "Momma, can a Yankee go to heaven?" "Don't ask foolish questions, son. Of course not."

Yankee dime: A kiss. "How 'bout a Yankee dime, sugar?"

Yankee shot: A Southern child's navel. "Momma what's this on my belly?" "That's where the Yankee shot you. That's yo Yankee shot."

Yarbs: Herbs. "Grandmaw's fixin' to

make a spring tonic out of roots and yarbs."

Yawl: A useful Southern word that is consistently misused by Northerners when they try to mimic a Southern accent, which they do with appalling regularity. Yawl is always plural because it means you-all, or all of you. It is never—repeat, never—used in reference to only one person. At least not by Southerners. "Where yawl goin'?"

Yonduh: In a particular direction. "That's a pretty house over yonduh on that hill."

Z

Zackly: Precisely. "Ah don't zackly know where he is."

Zat: Is that. "Zat yo dawg?"

Steve Mitchell,
a North Carolinian, is
a columnist for the
Palm Beach (Fla.) Post.

Sam C. Rawls,
a Florida cracker, is
the chief cartoonist
for the Palm Beach Post.

Both are lazy
and would rather go
bass fishing than work.